D1228633

Science Tools

Thermometers

by Adele Richardson

Consultant:
Dr. Ronald Browne
Associate Professor of Elementary Education
Minnesota State University, Mankato

Mankato, Minnesota

St. John's School Lower Library

First Facts is published by Capstone Press
151 Good Counsel Drive, P.O. Box 669, Mankato, Minnesota 56002
http://www.capstonepress.com

Copyright © 2004 by Capstone Press. All rights reserved.
No part of this publication may be reproduced in whole or in part, or stored in a retrieval system, or transmitted in any form or by any means, electronic, mechanical, photocopying, recording, or otherwise, without written permission of the publisher.
For information regarding permission, write to Capstone Press,
151 Good Counsel Drive, P.O. Box 669, Dept. R, Mankato, Minnesota 56002.
Printed in the United States of America

Library of Congress Cataloging-in-Publication Data
Richardson, Adele, 1966–
    Thermometers / by Adele Richardson.
        p. cm.—(First facts. Science tools)
    Summary: Introduces the function, parts, and uses of thermometers, and provides instructions for two activities that demonstrate how a thermometer works.
    Includes bibliographical references and index.
    ISBN 0-7368-2519-3 (hardcover)
    1. Thermometers—Juvenile literature. [1. Thermometers.] I. Title. II. Series.
QC271.4.R532 2004
681'.2—dc22   2003013403

Editorial Credits
Christopher Harbo, editor; Juliette Peters, designer; Deirdre Barton, photo researcher;
    Eric Kudalis, product planning editor

Photo Credits
Capstone Press/Gary Sundermeyer, 1, 4, 5, 6, 7, 8, 9, 11, 12, 13, 14, 15, 16, 17, 18
Capstone Press/GEM Photo Studio/Dan Delaney, cover
Corbis/Roger Ressmeyer, 20

1 2 3 4 5 6 09 08 07 06 05 04

Table of Contents

The Class Investigates

Mr. Walker's students want to know if black or white **reflects** more light. They believe the color that reflects more light will stay cooler.

The students wrap one jar with black cloth and one with white cloth. They fill the jars with water. A thermometer is put in each jar. They set the jars in a window.

Turn to page 19 to try this activity!

What Is a Thermometer?

Thermometers are tools that measure **temperature**. The liquid inside a thermometer rises when temperatures are warm.

Fun Fact:
The word "therm" means heat. The word "meter" means a tool for measuring.

The liquid inside the thermometer falls in colder temperatures. A thermometer in ice water shows a low temperature.

TAYLOR®

glass tube

scales

red alcohol

°F °C

Parts of a Thermometer

Most thermometers have a glass tube, **red alcohol**, and temperature **scales**. The glass tube keeps the red alcohol inside. Temperature scales are printed on the card holding the tube.

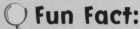 **Fun Fact:**
Many scientists use mercury thermometers to measure high temperatures. Mercury is a silver liquid metal.

A digital thermometer has a **sensor** on one end. The other end has a screen. The screen shows the temperature.

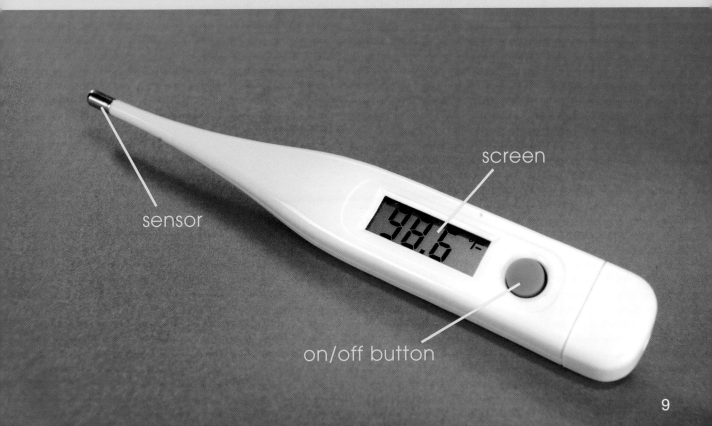

screen

sensor

on/off button

Fahrenheit and Celsius

Thermometers have **Fahrenheit** and **Celsius** scales. Water freezes at 32 degrees on the Fahrenheit scale. Water freezes at 0 degrees on the Celsius scale. This thermometer shows that 86 degrees Fahrenheit (86°F) is the same as 30 degrees Celsius (30°C).

 Fun Fact:
The Fahrenheit scale is used in the United States. Most other countries use the Celsius scale.

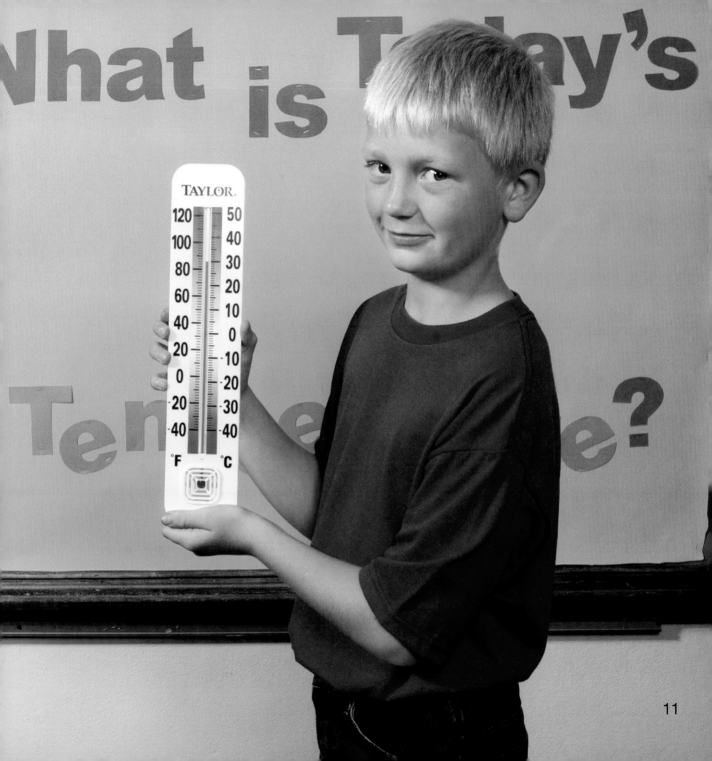

Thermometers in School

Students use thermometers to learn about temperature. These students are reading outdoor temperatures in sunny and shaded areas.

The students read a thermometer on a sunny playground. Then they see if the temperature is lower under a shady tree.

Other Uses for Thermometers

Nurses use thermometers. They test a person's body temperature. This girl's temperature is 101 degrees Fahrenheit (38.3 degrees Celsius). She has a fever.

Cooks use thermometers to make
sure meat is fully cooked. This cooked
chicken is 180 degrees Fahrenheit
(82 degrees Celsius). It is safe to eat.

Test the World around You

Hot water heaters heat the water that comes out of faucets. Water hotter than 120 degrees Fahrenheit (49 degrees Celsius) could burn your skin. How hot is the water from your faucets?

Try It!

What You Need

faucet   pencil
coffee cup   paper
thermometer

What You Do

1. Turn on the hot water on your faucet.
2. Let the water run for 20 to 30 seconds. Do not touch the water. It could be very hot.
3. Carefully fill a coffee cup half full with water.
4. Put the thermometer in the water. Wait until the thermometer's red line stops rising. Write down the temperature of the water.

What Did They Learn?

Mr. Walker's students believed the white jar would stay cooler. Do you think they were right? Let's find out.

Try It!

What You Need

black cloth	2 thermometers	2 jelly jars
white cloth	piece of paper	sunny window
masking tape	pencil	water

What You Do

1. Wrap the black cloth around one jar and tape it to the jar. Wrap the other jar with the white cloth the same way.
2. Fill each jar with water. Let the jars stand for 1 hour so the water can reach room temperature.
3. Place a thermometer in each jar.
4. On a piece of paper, write down the temperature of the water in each jar.
5. Place both jars in a sunny window.
6. Check the temperature of the water in each jar every 15 minutes for 1 hour. Write down the temperatures for both jars each time you check them.

Conclusions

Which jar's water warmed up the most? Light colors reflect more light than dark colors. The water in the white jar should be a few degrees cooler than the water in the black jar.

Many people believe Galileo Galilei made the first thermometer. In 1593, he invented a thermometer that had no number scale. It only showed temperature changes in the air. Bulbs filled with liquid rose or fell inside the thermometer as temperatures changed. People can still buy similar thermometers today.

What Do You Think?

1. On a hot, sunny summer day, you have a choice between wearing a white T-shirt or a black T-shirt. Which T-shirt would you wear if you wanted to stay cooler? Why?

2. Why is the temperature scale an important part of a thermometer?

3. Water heaters change the temperature of water. What other appliances in a house change the temperature of something?

4. The Sun gives us light and heat. Would a thermometer show a warmer temperature in a sunny area or a shady area?

Glossary

Celsius (SEL-see-uhss)—a scale for measuring temperature; water freezes at 0 degrees Celsius.

Fahrenheit (FA-ren-hite)—a scale for measuring temperature; water freezes at 32 degrees Fahrenheit.

red alcohol (RED AL-kuh-hol)—a liquid often used in thermometers; alcohol in thermometers is often dyed red so it is easy to see.

reflect (ri-FLEKT)—to return light from an object

scale (SKALE)—a series of numbers used to measure something

sensor (SEN-sur)—an instrument that detects physical changes in the environment

temperature (TEM-pur-uh-chur)—the measure of how hot or cold something is

Read More

Auch, Alison. *That's Hot.* Spyglass Books. Minneapolis: Compass Point Books, 2002.

Royston, Angela. *Hot and Cold.* My World of Science. Chicago: Heinemann Library, 2002.

Internet Sites

FactHound offers a safe, fun way to find Internet sites related to this book. All of the sites on FactHound have been researched by our staff.

Here's how:

1. Visit *www.facthound.com*
2. Type in this special code **0736825193** for age-appropriate sites. Or enter a search word related to this book for a more general search.
3. Click on the Fetch It button.

FactHound will fetch the best sites for you!

Index